MINERS

extreme jobs

Big Buddy BOOKS
Extreme Jobs

Sarah Tieck

ABDO
Publishing Company

VISIT US AT
www.abdopublishing.com

Published by ABDO Publishing Company, 8000 West 78th Street, Edina, Minnesota 55439.

Copyright © 2012 by Abdo Consulting Group, Inc. International copyrights reserved in all countries. No part of this book may be reproduced in any form without written permission from the publisher. Big Buddy Books™ is a trademark and logo of ABDO Publishing Company.

Printed in the United States of America, North Mankato, Minnesota.
062011
092011

 PRINTED ON RECYCLED PAPER

Coordinating Series Editor: Rochelle Baltzer
Contributing Editors: Megan M. Gunderson, BreAnn Rumsch, Marcia Zappa
Graphic Design: Marcia Zappa
Cover Photograph: *iStockphoto*: ©iStockphoto.com/lom.
Interior Photographs/Illustrations: *Alamy*: imagebroker (p. 15); *AP Photo*: AP Photo (p. 27), Roberto Candia (p. 21), Juan Karita (p. 17), National Park Service, File (p. 27); *Getty Images*: Bruce Forster (p. 5), National Geographic (p. 11), Tyler Stableford (p. 23); *Glow Images*: Peter and Georgina Bowater (p. 7), Raga Jose Fuste (p. 13), Jim Pickerell (p. 9), www.picturethepast.org.uk/Nottinghamshire County Council/Heritage-Images (p. 25); *iStockphoto*: ©iStockphoto.com/fstop123 (p. 30), ©iStockphoto.com/snapphoto (p. 30); *Photolibrary*: Bios (p. 13), Lineair (p. 15); *Shutterstock*: accesslab (p. 13), Bn Campos (p. 19), Darren J. Bradley (p. 19), Dan Breckwoldt (p. 25), cbpix (p. 5), Terry Davis (p. 29), Joe Gough (p. 13), Kodda (p. 15), Dmitri Meinik (p. 7), Zurijeta (p. 30).

Library of Congress Cataloging-in-Publication Data

Tieck, Sarah, 1976-
   Miners / Sarah Tieck.
      p. cm. -- (Extreme jobs)
   ISBN 978-1-61783-026-6
   1. Miners--Vocational guidance--Juvenile literature. 2. Miners--Health and hygiene--Juvenile literature. I. Title.
   HD8039.M6T54 2012
   622.023--dc23
                    2011017210

CONTENTS

MINING 101

What if you couldn't ride your bike, use a computer, or turn on the lights? These things are possible because of Earth's metals, **minerals**, and coal. Workers called miners **excavate** these natural **resources**.

Some miners work in surface mines. Others risk their lives to work thousands of feet underground. Now that's an extreme job!

Coal (*left*) is used for heating. Coal miners (*above*) often work underground.

FACT ALERT

Gold and diamonds often come from underground mines.

Mines are built around large **deposits** of valuable **resources**. The type of mine is based on the deposit's location and shape.

Some deposits are near Earth's surface. For these, pit mines, strip mines, and quarries are built.

Other deposits are far beneath Earth's surface. So, miners must dig with machines and use **explosives**. They work in tunnels and rooms deep underground.

Gold mines can be more than one mile (1.6 km) below Earth's surface.

Explosives help break apart rock and earth.

Underground miners go down into a mine to start their work. The mines are naturally very dark. Miners set up lights so they can see.

Inside mines, many spaces are large enough for trucks and other machines! Miners use machines to do much of their work. Still, they are covered in dust or mud by the end of most workdays.

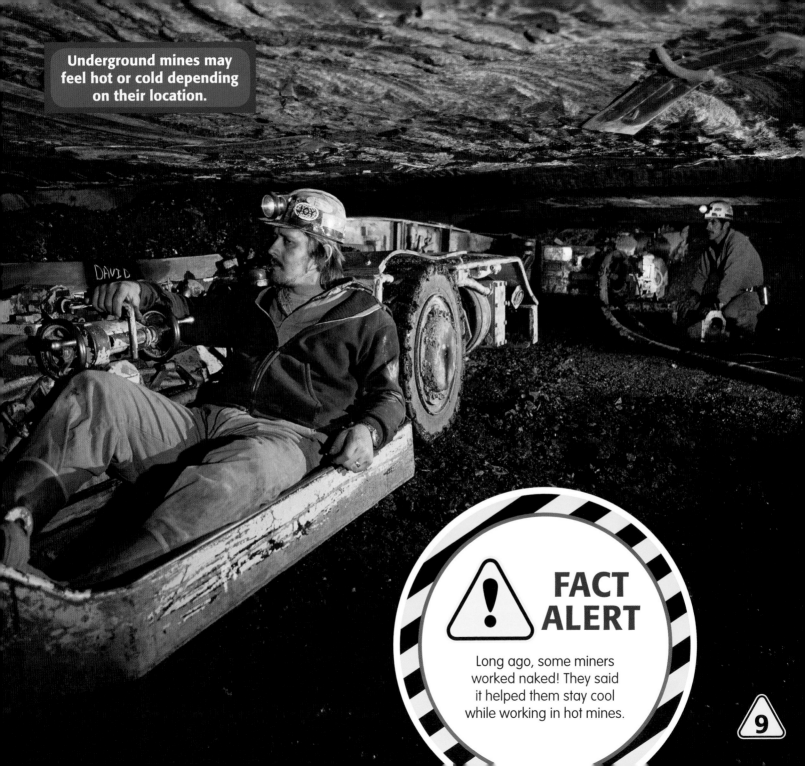

Underground mines may feel hot or cold depending on their location.

FACT ALERT

Long ago, some miners worked naked! They said it helped them stay cool while working in hot mines.

9

A DAY'S WORK

Most miners work for 8 to 12 hours at a time. This is called a shift. Many work for several days in a row. Then they have time off.

Miners have certain jobs to do. They may find, dig, sort, or send out parts of a **deposit**. Some miners build the mine. Others operate machines.

Some miners fix broken
tools or machines.

It takes a large number of people to keep a mine working safely. Scientists and **managers** often work outside the mine. But sometimes, they visit mines and work with miners.

After miners remove material, the valued parts are separated from the extra rock. Then, they are sold. People around the world use mined materials. These include coal, metals, and **minerals**.

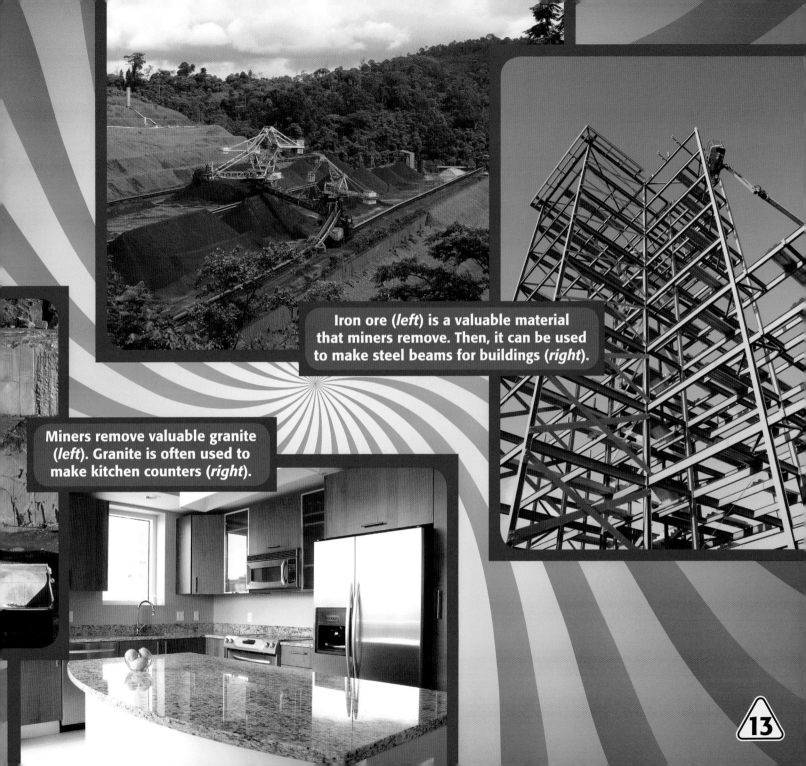

Iron ore (*left*) is a valuable material that miners remove. Then, it can be used to make steel beams for buildings (*right*).

Miners remove valuable granite (*left*). Granite is often used to make kitchen counters (*right*).

GEARING UP

Long ago, miners did much of their work by hand. Today, most work is done by machines. The machines cut rock and remove it from mines. Miners also use **explosives** to break apart rock.

To stay safe, miners wear heavy-duty clothes and hard hats. They must be very careful around powerful machines and tools. And, they watch out for falling rock.

Special drills help miners break apart rock.

Hard hats have headlamps. This lets miners shine light while keeping their hands free.

A bucket-wheel excavator is a type of digging machine. It allows miners to get more materials from a mine with less work.

BREATHE IN

Deep underground, the **air pressure** is greater than on Earth's surface. So as miners go down into a mine, the air feels heavier. This can make it harder to breathe.

Miners must be careful when going into and out of the mine. If the pressure changes too quickly, they can get sick. So they take care to go up and down slowly.

Human lung are filled with air pressure these parts

A miner's work often feels even harder because of the air pressure changes.

DANGER! DANGER!

Mining is very risky work. It has become safer in recent years. There are more laws and standards. And, tools and mining practices are better.

Still, accidents can trap or even kill miners. Underground mines can cave in or flood. They may blow up or fill with deadly gases. Miners can get serious wounds from accidents with tools, machines, or rock.

Abandoned mines are no longer used. They are very unsafe, so people should stay away from them.

FACT ALERT

Mines have gases and dust. These can make some miners sick.

19

If miners get trapped, **rescue** teams quickly get to work. They often must dig to reach the miners. Teams work long hours to get them out safely.

In 2010, 33 miners in Chile were rescued from a gold and copper mine. They had spent 69 days trapped underground! Can you see the rescued miner in the tube?

READY, SET, GO!

Miners with experience and training work with machines or **explosives**. New miners learn by helping the other miners.

Some mine workers have college **degrees** in science or another area. They may help locate **deposits**, plan mine work, or check conditions.

Most miners don't need college degrees. But, they must be strong and healthy.

THEN TO NOW

The first mines were made during prehistoric times. People dug holes to gather **minerals** for making weapons and tools.

In the 1400s, Europeans began mining coal and iron ore. Around the 1700s, these **resources** became more valuable. They helped heat homes and run machines in factories.

The pyramids of Egypt were built from stone mined in quarries.

FACT ALERT

Long ago, children as young as ten worked in mines! Later, laws were made to protect them from this unsafe work.

Early mines were very unsafe. Working conditions were hard, and many people were hurt or killed.

Then in 1848, the famous California gold rush started. Thousands of people traveled west to mine gold. They used pickaxes and shovels to search for gold.

Around the same time, people began mining silver, lead, and coal in the United States. Over time, mining became an important US industry.

Around 1915, zinc miners in Arkansas did much of their work by hand.

During the gold rush, people used pans and water to look for gold.

ABOVE GROUND

Mining can be unsafe. But, miners do important work. Their extreme job provides valuable **resources** to people and businesses. This improves lives around the world!

Miners must pay close attention to their work.

WHEN I GROW UP...

Explore parts of a miner's job now!

Miners know a lot about the rock they work with. What kind of rocks are there where you live?

Miners use many different tools. They may drill holes or put up beams in an underground room. Ask an adult to show you how they use drills and other tools.

Miners lift and move heavy objects such as rocks. To do this, they need to be very strong and healthy. Exercise and eat right so you can be strong and healthy, too!

IMPORTANT WORDS

air pressure (PREH-shuhr) the weight of air as it pushes on objects.

degree a title given by a college, university, or trade school to its students for completing their studies.

deposit mineral matter found in rocks or in the ground.

excavate (EHK-skuh-vayt) to carefully dig out material from the ground.

explosive a substance used to blow up something.

manager someone who directs the work of a person or a group.

mineral a natural substance. Minerals make up rocks and other parts of nature.

rescue (REHS-kyoo) to save from danger or harm.

resource a supply of something.

WEB SITES

To learn more about miners, visit ABDO Publishing Company online. Web sites about miners are featured on our Book Links page. These links are routinely monitored and updated to provide the most current information available.

www.abdopublishing.com

INDEX